To Stephanie

A very
special
Gal "

the Best
always

Tony Hart

BROOKLYN-ESE PROVERBS & CARTOONS

BROOKLYN-ESE PROVERBS & CARTOONS

BY

LAWRENCE S. HARTE

Lawrence S. Harte is solely responsible for the contents of this book,
and apologizes in advance if anything in it is not entirely original.

Illustrations by David McCoy, www.davetoons.com
Dustjacket by David McCoy and Peter Weisz
Design and formatting by Lynne Adams

ISBN: 978-0-9662602-8-1
LCCN: 2011925472

First edition. First printing.
Manufactured in the United States

Publisher's Cataloging-in-Publication Data
Harte, Lawrence S.
Brooklyn-ese proverbs and cartoons / by Lawrence S. Harte ;
illustrations by Dave McCoy.
p. cm.
ISBN: 978-0-9662602-8-1
1. Proverbs, American. 2. Brooklyn (New York, N.Y.).   I. McCoy, Dave,
ill. II. Title.
PN6426 .H53 2011
398.9—dc22
2011925472

White Poppy Press
34 Main Street #9
Amherst, MA 01002-2356
www.whitepoppypress.com

Dedication

This book is dedicated to all of the people who have had a relationship with Brooklyn and to all who would like to enjoy the spirit of Brooklyn.

It is my hope that when you read it, you will be able to

1. *laugh*
2. *say uhh-huh*
3. *smile, and*
4. *enjoy*

Introduction

At the age of nine, I asked my dad, "Why don't we root for the Yankees? They always seem to win."

My dad stood up, pointed his finger at my soon-to-be-big nose, and said, "Son, we live in Brooklyn. Our team is and always will be the Dodgers. Never forget that!"

I have never forgotten that!

Speaking of baseball, when I was a kid playing baseball in Brooklyn, my coach would say things that I thought were pretty funny. They usually came with some of his thoughts about life, and I learned that a humorous saying often has a deeper meaning.

I was smitten with the idea that behind a humorous saying or cartoon can be a lesson of life that we can enjoy, learn, and share with our children and friends.

I have tried to translate Brooklyn-ese into Harten-ese.

It is my hope that you will not have to go to Berlitz language school for a translation.

Acknowledgment

I would like to thank Kathy Phillips, who played the devil's advocate while I was working on this book, and sometimes had me in such a tizzy that I wasn't sure if I (or the proverbs and cartoons) was coming or going.

BROOKLYN-ESE PROVERBS & CARTOONS

It is said that he who *lives* with the classes *works* with the masses, and he who *works* with the classes *lives* with the masses.

Being spoon fed at an early age does not sharpen one's teeth.

Have the courage of your convictions.

When a child is confronted with a problem and asks himself, "What would my parents do?" — that is a parent's greatest compliment!

A practical person takes the headache out of headaches.

Some people were born with a silver spoon in their mouth. I was born with a plastic fork.

We are all a tapestry of our past, but we can throw it out and start a new one.

People don't usually change their minds after they've made up their minds (which takes about five minutes).

One tends to think that things that can be easily visualized are more likely to happen.

If we spend too much time retracing our old steps, we will never have time for new steps.

**I took a course in memory,
but I forgot what they said.**

Be a systems person. Look at both the whole and each individual part.

Focus on real solutions, not unreal problems.

   Successful people all have one thing in common: they focus and block out the everyday whispers of life.

In times of shock and despair, keep your eye on the mark.

Begin each morning with a "do" reminder so that it can be a "done" day.

**Success comes from
constant positive focus.**

People buy; you do not sell.

If you are sincerely enthusiastic, you can tell people where to go and they will say, "Great, I'll take two!"

There are always house rules. As in baseball and ice-cream, the home team gets the last lick.

Time stays forever; only man moves away.

Sometimes, people who seem overwhelming turn out to be underwhelming.

**The sun is always out,
but once in a while
the clouds are in the way.**

The next time you're feeling down, watch an old comedy (or just tickle yourself).

My father once said, "If you can keep your mouth shut, and open it only to smile, people will think you are a scholar and a gentleman."

Accent the positive. Eliminate negativity.

It takes a lot of dough to make a pizza.

Life is what you want it to be.

If you have lemons, make lemonade. Success comes from a positive mental attitude.

We should look internally, to ourselves, for financial and emotional guidance.

In investing, the little guy is like a barnacle on a whale, just going along for the ride.

Legalized bookmaking is where big banks and funds, in good times and in bad, can profit on both the buy and the sell.

Can you imagine if Democrats and Republicans could agree on what is best for their country and not their party?

Teach accountability to a child and she will be responsible as an adult.

 **Checks and balances are necessary in government and in our home.**

LIFE'S CHATTER

A Mother's Love

The only thing better than your children achieving your dreams is to do it yourself. My mother worked six days a week all her life so that she could offer me a better life. Once when I visited her in the nursing home, she told me, "I love you." But more importantly, when people walked by she said, "This is my son, the doctor." I had a tear in my eye.

A Novice Jewelry Clerk

When I was sixteen, I was a stock boy at a jewelry store. One day, the manager called me upstairs and said, "That lady can't decide which diamond ring to buy." I went over to the lady, knowing that I couldn't tell a diamond from a piece of glass. I listened patiently to the woman and, to my surprise, she bought a ring. The manager explained to me that he had felt she was going to walk out without a sale, so he'd had nothing to lose by giving me a chance.

The Hot Dog Story

Preparation is what life is about. One summer day at the age of fourteen, I was working at a fast-food restaurant called Nedicks. My job was serving hot dogs. I was so proud of myself for my sales pitch. I sold out. The problem was that it never occurred to me that I should bring up new hot dogs to put on the grill. I had no hot dogs to sell and my boss suggested I look for a new job.

Overbooked

How to get into a hotel. One can say to the booking person, "I know that there are 500 people who have booked into the hotel. You and I know that there is going to be at least one cancellation. What can you and I do so that, in the event that there is a cancellation, you will give it to me?

Stress is related to health. Less stress can add ten productive years of life, rather than sucking wind.

The diet that is good for one part of your body is good for all parts of your body.

The greatest failure is the failure of imagination.

Health is the fastest growing industry in the U.S., the only sickness that is doing well.

In college, I told my dad I was majoring in philosophy. He said, "Come home. I'll put you on a truck for fourteen hours a day." I changed my major.

**People who exercise their
bodies and brains get happier,
mentally and physically.**

As a kid, I had an idyllic life. I didn't expect anything. I didn't want anything. And I didn't get anything.

Make each day a challenge, rather than either a blessing or a curse.

Eating candy is a one-inch high and a two-inch low.

People can laugh *at* you as long as they are also laughing *with* you.

Have a reason for *doing* things. Have two reasons for *undoing* things.

Make life changes. The more you lose, the more you gain.

To the seller, it's food. But to you, the buyer, it's just dessert. You can always walk away from dessert.

Some people have role models; I was a bagel model.

If everything is important, nothing is important.

Weight loss belongs in the mind and ends in the body.

Tailors do well in times of big donuts and hot dryers.

**Tight clothes come from a
hot dryer or too many donuts.**

As a horse goes under low-lying branches with a rider of little experience, so is a person taken advantage of when he is not prepared for his new environment.

Necessity and accomplishment are the mother and father of invention.

How do you know when a task is finished? When the bell rings.

Newspaper headlines are usually the same. Only the dates and names change.

He who speaks with forked tongue cuts up mouth.

Many habits stay with us. The way you eat when you're young may be the way you eat when you're old.

People should not comment on their direction or speed, but only on the consequences of their actions.

It is obvious what *not* to do, but it is not obvious what *to* do.

If one thinks of doing something, do it immediately, before the little gremlin says, "What was I supposed to do?"

The new epidemic: stress in suburbia.

Maturity is when the shade on the light bulb begins to fade.

**The advantage of a tough
morning workout is that nothing
can faze you the rest of the day.**

The door to happiness opens outwards.

Be a tank with lots of fuel. Keep going in a happy, persistent, tenacious, and relentless way.

People who are light on their toes do not have their heels stuck in cement.

You are never so different from your competitors—it can be a difference of human experience.

The only advantage of looking back is you will trip on your shoelaces.

Sometimes getting to your workout is the real workout.

LIFE'S CHATTER

Maxwell's Plum

Years ago, when we could not get into Maxwell's Plum, a famous restaurant, one of us went up to the maitre d' and said, "I bet you twenty bucks you can't get us in within ten minutes." He responded, "You lose."

The Right Price

A Midwestern farmer went to a local store to buy a new tractor and balked at the price of a John Deere. The manager responded, "If you want something guaranteed to last or if you need service for repairs, I am just minutes away!" A personal relationship can be a worthwhile investment.

Pee Wee Reese

Pee Wee Reese, the great Brooklyn Dodgers Hall of Famer, once saw me pitching. He asked me what I wanted to do when I grew up. I told my mom what he said. My mother gave me a kiss and said, "Son, study, because it is not going to be baseball."

Health Reform

Some people order the drugs.
Some people use the drugs.
The rest of us pay for the drugs.

The Race

It is not how you start the race, but how you finish it. As a kid, I would run from the starting gate, sprinting, and at the end of the 440 I was exhausted. I had nothing left in my gas tank.

My dad once told me, "Sometimes it isn't the hare who wins the race, but the turtle. Conserve your energy for that final spurt. Use the rabbit as a guide to stay close and then pour it on in the final bell lap."

In the wintertime in Florida, it can be drop-dead gorgeous. In the North, though, it can be drop-dead cold. If any colder we'd be dead.

Life is a circle—we begin with soft foods and end with soft foods.

As we mature, we switch from salt to salt-free foods.

It is not how old your friends are, but how young their attitudes are.

Bears and birds have it right: bears sleep in the winter and birds go south.

**Anybody over fifty who shovels
snow should have excellent
health and life insurance.**

People with too much time on their hands transfer the time to their butts!

Work is the definition of movement, so when someone says, "I worked hard all day," you can wonder, "Did you also move?"

I never use medicine for my athlete's foot because if I did, I would be taking away the only place that I am an athlete.

Never go to sleep angry.

Like and be who you are.

**I didn't do a darned thing today,
but I sure am tired from doing it.**

He who plays with fire may need someone else's hands to handle the fire.

Begin with a smile and follow with a question about the other person—and they're yours forever.

The nature of man has always been the same. It's how civilized we take our nature that makes us different.

Assume nothing and never go against your gut.

My mother lived in a nursing home. She would call, and no one would respond. One day, she called 911. From then on, whenever she called the aides came pronto.

**Bullies are not popular.
Stand tall and gain respect.**

Try to relate to others in a way that can bring out their best.

We can only offer our children the *opportunity* of a lifetime, not a *guarantee* of a lifetime.

If one can't convince with words, dazzle with footwork.

My Uncle Lou lived to 106, drinking light tea six times a day, which cleansed his soul and body.

Schools should teach civic and cultural involvement.

It takes more effort to frown than to smile. Smiling makes us look better and shows fewer wrinkles.

There are equals and there are equals
in this world.

Whether you agree or not, getting
someone else's view can broaden your mind
and your happiness.

Don't make little things into big things
unless they are fun things.

How do I know who I am until I hear
what I say?

Hang out with people who are positive and you will be less negative.

Try to analyze potential problems and anticipate answers before the problems become chronic.

We should not try to fix our problems on the fly with a Band-Aid.

You can get further with a kind word if people can hear and understand you.

People will die for an emotional principle rather than reason for peace.

If you can keep your head while others around you are losing theirs, you will live longer.

Be careful who you thumb your nose at. You may hurt their feelings and your gut.

LIFE'S CHATTER

Happiness

As a kid in Brooklyn, a peddler came to our alley each week saying, "Buy cash, clothes." He was always happy.

I asked him, "How can you be so happy, walking all day in all kinds of weather with a heavy knapsack on your back?"

He said, "I get up every day and am on the right side of the dirt. I make each day as if it was going to be my last—fun and enjoyable."

Relationships

If you want to understand another person, you must see them with *their* eyes, hear them with *their* ears, and feel them with *their* heart.

Experience has shown that the people who are best at human relationships are those who have this ability.

Repeat, Repeat

I never could understand why my parents kept saying things twice to me. I thought they were getting senile.

However, as I grew up, I got into the habit of repeating directions twice, as they do in a hospital. The doctor says, "Scalpel," and the nurse repeats, "Scalpel."

The advantage of saying it twice is that you might get it right and not screw up.

The disadvantage is that the patient could become a bumbling idiot.

If you want to teach children, have them look up the facts themselves rather than doing the work for them.

Winning is great, but as in the Olympics, there are gold, silver, and bronze medals. How many of us would settle for bronze?

If the other person is better, they may beat you. But never beat yourself.

I like myself more than you like yourself.

By the age of nine, most children have developed most of their character traits.

**If you treat me
as I ought to be,
I WILL be!**

A military option can prepare one battle in advance. A diplomatic option prepares years in advance.

People fire themselves.

Give employees equity and they will have the same enthusiasm as the boss.

If the crowd goes one way, go the other way. There is less traffic and you will get there faster.

**In facing up to the problems
of today, we sow the seeds
of the joys of tomorrow.**

The reason people double-space is so that they can read between the lines.

It is not the politics of the person, but rather the value of their politics.

Growing up in Brooklyn, there were two kinds of pigeons—stool pigeons and dead pigeons.

A man was stopped by a policeman. "Didn't you see the red light?" the officer asked him. He answered, "I saw the light. I just didn't see you!"

President Teddy Roosevelt spoke softly, but people noticed the big stick.

**Incentives work, but you still
need both a carrot and a stick.**

One's greatest enemy is not a person who is open to change, but one who does not want change.

Common cents make uncommon dollars.

I was once in a country with strong government control. The employees said, "The government pretends to pay us and we pretend to work."

Cartoons are like a Rorschach test. Every person will have a different interpretation.

Titanic ship syndrome: People on the high side of life refuse to accept the despair of the low side.

People who are flexible are happier.

He who says practice makes perfect
is 100 percent wrong. *Good* practice
makes perfect.

In sports, as in life, people with stamina and
a will to win usually overcome sheer talent.

Good athletes have one thing in common:
they focus.

If you are tenacious, persevering, and
diligent, the world will be yours.

A good athlete always keeps moving, even
when standing still.

A professional makes new mistakes every day. An amateur makes the same mistake every day.

People can think but must have the courage
of their convictions to act.

There is a recipe for getting a desired result:
     tincture of necessity
     tincture of thinking outside the box
     pound of chance-taking

A great salesperson is someone who
can have a buyer accept both a want
and a need.

Great leaders have the ability to modify
behavior, hopefully in a positive way.

"You can take a horse to water, but you can't make him drink" is 100 percent wrong! You can salt the horse's oats.

LIFE'S CHATTER

Communication

I remember lecturing in French on a serious topic of growth and development when I was in Paris. The harder I tried, the more I had the audience in hysterics. They thought I was Maurice Chevalier. I learned that it's not what you say, it's how you say it.

The Family

Growing up, I had little patience for family gatherings. Listening to Uncle Waldo's tired, boring jokes over and over again, and hearing about Aunt Zelda's recipe for greasy chicken soup made me want to gag. I got annoyed when Grandpa Aaron pinched my cheek and gave me a nickel. To this day I have indentations in my cheeks from the love abuse.

However, as I grew up and had my own, I began to recognize the importance of family. The family was there when you were down—and the family was there to put a spark plug under you to get you going.

Compound Interest of a Mensch

If you could try to do one good deed every day, your life would be overly filled with the abundance of joy and happiness that you have tried to give to your fellow man. This is the greatest blessing of compound interest.

Wearing Yourself Out

I was always working double- and triple-time when I was a kid. My father said, "You only have one set of gears, and once they wear out, so do you."

I should have listened to him! I worked double- and triple-overtime and now, in my later years, I am literally a bionic person. Knees, hips, ankles. The only thing that is original is the brain (but it seems to have less cells than it once had).

Some people want to watch what happens. Some people want to make it happen. Most of us wonder what the heck happened.

He is the bundle of irrelevancy.

Did you ever hear someone say, "honestly speaking" or "truthfully speaking"? What comes to your mind?

If you took out weather, food, and movies, a lot of conversations would be silent.

A complicated mind is full of intellectual manure. An uncomplicated mind is full of random diarrhea.

Most people talk about nothing because it doesn't require much thought.

Stop trying to be a perfectionist.
You will be giving everybody a headache,
including yourself.

If people trust you, they will take your
advice.

Waiting on tables can be a prerequisite
for relating to people.

Man is his own worst enemy and
dog is his best friend.

Tacking, as in sailing, can get you to your
goal even when the wind is not behind
your back.

To be successful, put your nose to the grindstone.

If education is expensive, what is the cost of ignorance?

If someone says, "Thank you," say, "You're welcome," or, "My pleasure." Never say, "No problem," because that infers a problem.

If a lad is approached at a restaurant table, he should stand up, unless he has a spaghetti face and ketchup hands.

Don't let uncontrolled emotion get in the way of logical rhetoric.

Execute with excellence.

The value of an education: People can take your money and your clothes, but they can't take your mind.

Modern education is based on memory for exams and then forgetting everything right after the test.

Renaissance education was based on understanding the value of a subject and then sharing it with society and your children.

It is not the school, it is the student.

The best teacher of children is usually a Dutch uncle or aunt type of person. These people offer objective love, love without sentimentality.

A child will have the greatest development when the family puts off instant gratification for present hard work.

What you memorize, you are bound to forget. What you understand is yours forever.

Great accomplishments come from little steps and big planning.

Wars and many of life's challenges are won not by brilliant strategy but by making fewer mistakes.

In most events in life, if you give people a chance to make a mistake, they will usually oblige you.

Teach children music, art, and good habits by age three, before they learn to say *no no no*.

People should have the opportunity to question. We need these pebbles in the waters of history.

People who climb the highest mountains begin by planning the smallest steps.

If you are a true leader, you will not be pulled down by others.

People will look up to other people who have charisma and the guts to stand up for their opinions.

People will respect you for your attitude and your mental strength.

To be a true statesman requires the ability to lead the masses even when they are half-cocked.

In order to cut down strength, we must create doubt.

 **A true leader might have to step on toes to get people's attention.**

LIFE'S CHATTER

Excuses

Years ago, when I was working in a psychiatric hospital (not as a patient), all of the employees were late one day and the supervisor asked us why.

Most of us said it was that construction in front of the building had made us go around to the back, but one lad from Mississippi said, "I was late because I didn't allow myself enough time."

How many times have we been late for work because it was "snowing out"?

The real question is why didn't we get up earlier?

The successful person rarely, if ever, gives an excuse.

Cheap

I am not big on trading posts, but some people never learn. I guess that's me.

The family once took a trip to Arizona in

an un-air-conditioned car. (I'm cheap.) After driving some 200 miles, I was cajoled into visiting an Indian trading post and forced to look at antique jewelry that the guy had just finished making.

I asked, "How much?"

He said, "$10."

But I'd had training in negotiations, so I said, "Can you give me a good buy?"

He looked at the jewelry, looked at me, put out his hand to shake, and said, "Good-bye"!

Western Union

When I was working at Western Union as a kid, I would come to work in a T-shirt. A co-worker who had less money than I (which was not easy) came to work in a shirt, tie, and jacket. He was always smiling and the people he delivered to were apparently so impressed that they tipped him far more than anyone else (including me). His smile lit up the night sky.

Try to relate to others in a way that brings out their best.

Executives spend so much energy working out. It is their way to keep their muscles limber on the corporate ladder.

Elected officials are so involved in running for office that they have little time to find out where the office is.

People expend so much energy fighting to go somewhere, they have little energy left to go anywhere.

The art of politics is where I have something to sell and you have something to buy.

Know where the pennies are, and the dollars will follow.

The ladder to success involves pulling the top guy down and kicking the guy on the rung below.

In negotiation, when you negotiate with yourself, you lose.

In successful negotiations, it is not the details of the sale but rather the presentation of the art of the deal.

In the Air Force, he who packs the parachutes should choose last and jump first.

Gertrude Stein once said, "This is no answer, and *that* will be the answer."

Whether it's weather, politics, or events that happen in life, she was right on the money.

In negotiation, he who speaks first loses.

There is only an excuse for doing *something*. There is no excuse for doing *nothing*.

If a task takes overly long, the odds are that it will be repeated.

Don't ask people how they are, unless you have time on your hands and an understanding soul.

When you are healthy, work double-time to make up for the half-time when you are ill.

**There is rarely an excuse
for giving an excuse.**

As a kid, time was forever. As an adult, there is never enough time.

If one thinks about a present subject too long, it becomes past tense.

By filling up every moment with multitask minutes, there is no time to smell the roses.

In competition neutralize the other's strengths and excel in yours.

Life is relative. If everything is happy, what is sad?

**People are time-starved
but not food-starved.**

When trying to arouse an audience, speak slowly in short simple sentences that are repeatable.

If you ask a question, you are engaging a person. You may not like their answer, but there is room for dialogue.

Humility comes before civility.

What comes out of your mouth when you are young can kick you in the butt when you are an adult.

Instead of saying, "We have a problem," say, "We have an opportunity."

**God gave us
one mouth to ask questions
and two ears to listen.**

Most people, if they sneeze once, they sneeze twice. So say "God bless you" twice on the first sneeze.

It is not how smart you are but how you use your smarts.

A master can teach his disciple everything, but certain things can only come with the experience of time.

If you are in a 10-story burning building on top of a swirling ocean, jump into the water. At least you have a chance of being saved.

It's better to see it TWICE than miss it ONCE.

LIFE'S CHATTER

Boring

I used to be with a group of people who had the same views on everything. It was emotional and intellectual boredom.

After a while, it was like going to a party of one and hearing myself talk through others.

Self Esteem

Treat people the way you want them to be. I remember a small skinny kid with no self-esteem who came to my office, and over the years I saw how his parents built him up by giving him little ways to achieve success.

The combination of straight teeth and many small accomplishments apparently made him feel good about himself, physically and emotionally. He is now CEO of a major company.

Geometry

Geometry is a basis for success. Many students complain that they will never use geometry in life, so why learn it? Geometry is a discipline. By disciplining your mind and yourself, you can learn to discipline others.

Brooklyn Kids

Brooklyn kids can be aggressive. It is not that they are more aggressive than other kids, but they are taught that you might get only one shot at the target, so why not take advantage by going first?

Why Change?

When I first opened my practice in town, I got involved with an effort to change from private septic systems to a public sewer system. An old-timer said, "My grandfather had septic, my parents had septic, and I'll continue to have septic." He was right, and for many years the town continued to have septic systems.

A fact is more important than potential.

Honey, I know where I am *not* going, so why should I ask for directions?

To admit being wrong is to admit being enlightened.

Most people come to a meeting without an open mind. It is the job of the speaker to unlock some of the gates.

In speaking to people, it's not what you say to them, it's what it means to them.

 **People hear but don't listen.**

You can relate to people, and they, in turn, will relate to you because you are both on the same wavelength.

You are understanding each other's feelings. It is win-win.

A friendship that is challenged is a true friendship.

Forgive yourself: Quiet guilt does not go with happiness.

In real estate rentals, better to get something rather than nothing.

Hate is not the opposite of love. Indifference is.

Never go to sleep angry.

Always forgive, never forget.

How to stop a long-winded person: Interrupt them by repeating their last sentence, and smile.

Now it's your turn to be long-winded.

People as they mature lose height but gain stature.

**Salutary Neglect:
Lack of personal
communication is the source
of a soured friendship.**

If you don't take care of yourself, you can't take care of others.

"Try" is not a word. "Will" is a word. "Good" is not a word. "Great" is a word.

Can we dream the impossible dreams and try to reach the unreachable stars?

Storytelling with a PowerPoint presentation can keep the eyes open and the body awake.

I think it's time for me.

When you have dreams, you have love
and a future.

A sense of good feeling is a combination
of altruism and selflessness.

Men may have common sense.
Women have common sense and
uncommon-scents!

Give people examples of how great they are.
Never just say they are great.

It's not the meal, it's the company.

A person who comes onto you in a hurry leaves you in a bigger hurry.

In meeting someone, make it positive and memorable by the words you use and the demeanor you exhibit.

In speaking to people or audiences, speak not only to the "yesses" but also the "maybe's" and the "no's."

I want to share something with you, rather than tell you something.

Magic is an illusion and a delusion.

At fourteen I was a Boy Scout. Then I turned girl scout.

LIFE'S CHATTER

Success

There is nothing in this world that you can't do if you're willing to pay the price. The price is not necessarily brains, but it helps. The price is not necessarily wealth, but it helps. Price is also tenacity and good luck.

Problems

There are problems but there are also solutions. The solutions are not in the changing winds but how we set our sails to get where we want to go. Success comes from vision and leadership.

Rancid Butter

We have opportunities in life. Often, there is a time sequence when we have to use this information. It's like butter. If it's kept out, it becomes rancid. There is a time and place for doing things. Make sure that the day and time don't pass by and the butter doesn't get rancid.

Kids

When I was chair of the Public Health Council of New Jersey, we looked into diet and exercise for our youth. To our dismay, we discovered that kids thought exercise was texting and playing video games (with a candy bar next to them for energy). They were breaking a sweat on their fingers.

Habits

I used to scratch my nose. My mother said, "Stop that—or it will become a habit and stay with you even when you're older." To this day, when I speak to a large audience, I often tell them I have something important to share and that they should pay attention. Later, when I review the video of the speech, I'm surprised to see that I scratched my nose, and in the back of my head I hear my mother saying, "I told you so!"

Questions are our friends.

As a lifeguard, always try to save people. If there is a choice, make sure you're the person left to tell about it.

Teams, like orchestras, have different personalities and instruments that combine for a great performance.

Baby animals can be as loving as any child, but they all grow up.

We should celebrate Thanksgiving Day every day of our life.

**Saying "I love you"
to the people who count
offers the greatest dividend
through the years.**

Family is what life and what love are about.

Facts and figures do not convey. Human experiences convey.

The limbs of a family tree come from the nourishment of its roots.

There are three types of life problems:
1. Let the small take care of themselves
2. Man can take care of the middle ones
3. Give God a chance on the big ones.

People, like bees, can spread the pollen of beauty.

**The grand essentials are:
a royal flush of life, to have and to hold.**

If you want someone to be your friend, ask them to do a favor that is do-able.

Man was put on earth not to be a spectator but to be a participant giving greater fruit than was given to him.

A child should be taught to stand up, look 'em in the eye, and give a firm handshake.

One can decrease misunderstanding in communication by using a noun instead of a pronoun.

The smile of a child is a universal language.

It doesn't take much to make someone happy.

People who are full of themselves have no time for love or life.

A facilitator is a person who can encourage people to do the very things they said they couldn't or wouldn't do previously.

People wish their own present and future on themselves by saying, "This is not my day."

Imagination and perspiration go hand in hand.

Make a good day, and you will have a good day.

Genius is inventing a rocket launcher or airplane. Insanity is going up in one without fuel.

People create their own reality.

Make each day a challenge, rather than a blessing or a curse.

Some of the smartest people in mental health facilities are there because they could not function in society.

**The difference between
insanity and genius is a fine line.**

Unless you ask the right question, you won't get the right answer.

A memoir is a series of data that we think, or hope, happened in our past.

The way to a sounder sleep: Be mindless at bedtime and let someone else fight your battles.

With a little rejection, there is an impetus for emotional growth.

Everybody needs an advocate, especially if they are under the weather or under the bar.

**Some people don't know
if they're coming or going.**

LIFE'S CHATTER

Hot Air

Life is like a balloon—you get a great deal of built-up air in a balloon, and unless you do something the balloon will burst, physically or emotionally.

So it is important that from time to time you have ways of letting out air and maintaining the balloon so it can fly in the sky and ride on the water. Otherwise, it will burst.

Good Deal

Years ago I met a man who was the president of a large inexpensive clothing outlet in the Northeast. I said to him, "I'm thinking of opening up a wine and cheese shop in a very high-class, fancy area." He laughed and said, "Why don't you open it up near my stores, in modest areas? You'll find that you'll make more net—and you'll have less aggravation and more fun."

Memory

Try to put things, i.e. eyeglasses and keys, in the same place every time. But if you misplace them, check your present surroundings first. Oftentimes, your glasses are on top of your head and well, yes, you left your keys in the car. If you misplace your glasses, check the top of your head.

Why Brooklyn Kids Should Do Well in the Submarine Service

Through their early years, they were used to turning their necks, and keeping their eyes and ears open to the environment around them. They used their heads as periscopes. It was a cultural means of survival.

An error of commission: when you try something and it doesn't come out.

An error of omission: when you try nothing and it doesn't come out.

It is better to try and lose but have a chance to win.

When you believe in yourself, others will believe in you.

Take a deep breath and jump in the water. You might like it.

**Life is a risk–reward ratio.
Unless you are prepared to
lose, you will never win.**

The Mr. Magoo Merrily Driving Syndrome is oblivious to the external environment, leaving a path of turmoil around us.

You may believe in a cause, but is it worth dying for? Think at least twice.

People who never get their feet wet, never get their head straight.

A child who hangs out with adults learns fast. An adult who hangs out with young people stays young.

**People look but they don't see.
You might be right,
but the car is usually left.**

The difference between a want and a need: I want a Mercedes, but do I need it?

Grandparents have the opportunity to give their kin love today and a clean environment tomorrow.

People who are into themselves find it difficult to give of themselves.

The geopolitical future of the world depends on our sacrifices today.

A legacy to our children: We have a choice—we can be part of the problem or part of the solution.

Price alone depreciates the product.

A good deal is where both sides felt they could have had a better deal.

Value is in the mind and the pocket of the beholder.

How to read people: Stop, look, and listen.

There is no free lunch. There is always a tax and the tip.

**You get what you pay for,
if you're lucky.**

As a kid, I did hand-stands. As an adult, I do foot-stands.

When I was twenty, I wanted to save the world. At forty, I wanted to save half of my wife's salary.

I have tried to learn some seven languages, including English. I am still trying to learn those seven languages, including English.

Be careful what you wish for. You may want to change your wish.

As a kid, every day was forever.

I wish I had the energy today that I thought I had when I was twenty.

On grandchildren
Enjoy their milestones, whatever they are.
Don't look for perfection.
Try to catch them doing something right.
Teach them to embrace their strengths
    and accept their weaknesses.
Keep thy mouth closed and thy wallet open.

When to retire? When one does not need work to define one's self.

Poetry helps one problem-solve.

Years ago I was on top of things. Now I am one of those things.

Retirement is what you make of it.

LIFE'S CHATTER

You Get What You Pay For

Before the onset of automatic pin set-up in bowling, I had a job setting up the pins after every frame. One guy was such a lousy tipper that I moved the pins in the wrong direction. The son of a gun never got a strike!

Laughter

In his book on laughter and its effect on illness, Norman Cousins said that there's no guarantee that you will be cured by laughter, but it will add to the quality of life and getting the best out of each day.

Man

What has four legs by light of day, two legs by heat of noon, and three legs by sunset?

Four legs when he is crawling in the morning of his life, two legs when he is walking strongly at adulthood, and three with a cane in the sunset of his life.

Speeding

If you really want to speed, keep the brights on, blink them on and off, get behind a speeding ambulance, and hope you won't need its services.

The Sea

People say the Mediterranean is a sea of glass. In stormy weather, it is a sea of broken glass.

They say that time flies.
Possibly time stays and we fly.

If you do not leave time to smell the roses,
people will smell the roses over you.

Every time you stop, take a look around
and hear and see the beauty of life.

Laugh and cry each day, but laugh more.

Get closer to the rose, even if you get stuck
once in a while.

**Life is a short walk—
enjoy each day.**

Things are not always as they appear. What appears at the start may disappear at the end.

Some people are oblivious to the external environment. They live in their own internal environment.

People who start out as the fun of the party quite often end as the flop of the party.

You can't move the mountain, but you can climb it.

It's not how you start in life, it's how you finish.

In communication and presentation, think and have the courage to act on your conviction.

Give it your best before you rest.

By seeing the world, you get a different feeling when you come home.

People who are ankylosed in their thoughts are frozen in time.

You can get on the train of life or watch it go by.

If someone writes to you, write them back. If someone calls you, call them back. If someone ignores you, you have choices.

In politics, like everything else, you need basics. You have to tackle and block.

If people hate your guts, don't agitate them any further.

Vultures live off the carcasses of deals gone astray.

People who retrace their footsteps do not have time for new footsteps.

Lawyers can wound a deal by trying to cut a deal.

There are two ways to win at a casino:
1. Don't bet
2. Own the casino

A Brooklyn bet: "I bet I can give you the score of the game before it starts." (The answer is always 0-0.)

Breakfast is the best meal of the day to get you invigorated mentally and physically.

On Sunday, we spend a few hours watching football, living vicariously.

Sunday is a man's soap opera.

With a woman, a man is going to lose. It's better to lose fast and graciously. It then becomes a win/win.

Too much logic gets in the way of joy.

Man is a hunter. It is too bad that he is a bad shot.

The more I work out, the more my bones turn to arthritis and my muscles to fat.

The mind is willing, but the body can't follow.

 **Middle-aged men act like dogs—
they chase but can't catch.**

If we constantly rehash the past, we will never get the opportunity to enjoy the present.

Never, never grow old. We should always have a bit of Peter Pan in us.

At a reunion, my friend said, "We were the best athletes!" I said, "We were?" My kids said, "You were?"

There is a rule of the swimming pool: If you are passed twice, you must move over. With me, that's the shower.

We honor our veterans, but should we not also sacrifice for them?

One may have a glorious past.
But the future is unknown.
So enjoy the present.

It is better to go through life trying—
and sometimes falling down—than saying,
If only....

**I bloodied my nose and
I skinned my knees, but I did it....**